Praise for Dodici Azpadu

"Dodici Azpadu's *Cloak* is the cinematic view of the life of an outsider growing up in a Sicilian Arab family fresh from Ellis Island, unlearning a mother's language and learning that their nationality is 'American.' Each scene is rich in detail and emotion, from an infant bed, 'a dresser drawer softened with towels,' to heading out into America 'to commit the crime of my life,' wearing ties and living nonbinary long before the term was coined. A jazz singer's 'I can't make you love me' to the poet becomes '*I* can't make the world love *me*.' Read *Cloak*. It's a gripping movie of a book."

— Mary Oishi, Albuquerque Poet Laureate Emerita, author of **Sidewalk Cruiseship**

"*Cloak* speaks of how queer people of color survive their families and social barriers with dignity intact. There is not a whine or poor-me anywhere, but there is a good deal of in-your-face. These poems take me back, and they offer a roadmap for today. Everyday spirituality is a special secret in this treasure chest."

— Linda Tillery, musician and producer

CLOAK

The Margaret Randall Poetry Series

El vuelo interminable / The Never-Ending Flight
   Eduardo Joly

Cloak
   Dodici Azpadu

CLOAK

The Margaret Randall Poetry Series #2

Dodici Azpadu

Casa Urraca Press
ABIQUIÚ

Copyright © 2026 by Dodici Azpadu

All rights reserved.

Thank you for supporting authors and artists by buying an authorized edition of this book and respecting all U.S. and other relevant copyright laws by not reproducing, scanning, or distributing any part of it in any form without express written permission from the publisher, except as permitted by fair use. You are empowering artists to keep creating, and Casa Urraca Press to keep publishing, books for readers like you who actually look at copyright pages.

This work of poetry contains references to real people and events. Some details may have been changed for privacy reasons and for creative license.

This book and its components are human-authored and human-designed without the use of artificial intelligence. No part of this work may be used to train AI technologies or develop machine learning language models, or for similar purposes, without the express written permission of the publisher.

Author photograph by Nancy Meyer
Cover photograph by Margaret Randall.
Set in Nobel and Odile.

29 28 27 26   1 2 3 4 5 6 7

First edition

The Margaret Randall Poetry Series #2

ISBN: 978-1-956375-50-3
Library of Congress Control Number: 2026930660

CASA URRACA PRESS

an imprint of Casa Urraca, Ltd.
casaurracapress.com

For my dear one
without whom this book would not exist.

Contents

Paper Trail

3	Silvio in Cinnamon
6	Ancestor Hash
8	Old, Old Country
9	Immigrant Haberdasher
10	Liz
12	Here and There
13	Paper Trail
14	Sleep Map
15	If You Must Speak
16	Guinea
19	House Storm
20	Yogi
21	Auld Lang Syne
22	Hooked Semitic Nose

Indigestible Memories

25	Weathered
26	Alumnae Class of '64
27	Golden Gate
28	Loaded Words
29	Business Tripping
32	SF/ABQ
33	Torch Song
34	Figment
35	Cloak
37	Remedial Science
38	Doctor Illusions
39	Touching
40	Clueless
41	Indigestible Memories

Ruins

45　Haikus for Dead Friends
46　Buried
47　Nakba
48　WhatsApp
49　Rubble
50　The Chair
51　Texas Pastor
53　Triangle
54　Troubled Sleep Ghazal

Good Life in Hard Times

57　Tennis at Winter's Edge
59　Midnight Stop
60　Mesas and Canyons
61　Fire Danger
63　Scotch and Buddha
64　White Horse
66　Holidays
67　Space Junk
68　Los Ojos
70　Summer Squash
72　Cold Mountain Morning
73　Al Fresco
74　On a Beach in Mazatlán

Life Lines

77 Iberian Scribe
78 Routine
79 Pens and Inks
80 Wet Ink
81 Contrails
82 Like an Ass

Lagniappe

85 Graveyard Relatives
87 Mediterranean Coast
88 Not a Trace

91 *Acknowledgments*
93 *About the author*
95 *The Margaret Randall Poetry Series*

PAPER TRAIL

Silvio in Cinnamon

Silvio in cinnamon suit and fedora
walks from Red Hook Projects

to work at moonrise. He plays piano
in a brownstone. Madam in

a feather boa collects money
at the door of the parlor floor

and serves watered-down
drinks; poses girls for dancing or

for coupling in rooms upstairs.

§

Silvio's hairless brown chest
uncovered, he sits

at the white metal table
with self-storing leaves;

in a drawer for utensils
is a deck of cards.

His father's Beretta with its silencer
is part of the table setting.

§

In a handheld grill,
Silvio's presumptive wife,
turns meat over the gas stove flame.

Their barefoot grandchildren
stop playing under the table

and move stone figures around
his pointy-toed butterscotch shoes.

A mysterious, taciturn man, some say
he choked to death on a bone.

The garrote story came after
the Beretta moved to the next generation.

§

Silvio's widow rocks in her chair
every day at the iron lattice window

in a South Brooklyn basement flat.
Ladies' oxfords, heavy stockings,

long black coats pass by:
Gianna's world view.

She lives on Home Relief
and money her daughters

secret to her. She speaks Sicilian,
not Italian, very little English.

She is free to go outside,
but seldom does.

Her wrap around housedress
hides a pocketful of pistachios.

The shells dyed red from Atlantic Avenue
Arab vendors stain her fingers,

the palm of her curled fist,
the shape of her frown.

Ancestor Hash

Gianna obscures ancestors
I eventually track

out of a hash of questions
I struggle with

her cultural suspicions
about telling anyone anything.

When I access the 1950 census,
I imagine a woman

in a gray gaberdine suit
with papers on her lap

shy of resting her arms
on the kitchen oil cloth.

Exhausted by contradictions,
the census-taker gives up

asking the illiterate
old lady to name and number

who lives in her house.
She leaves the garlic infused

basement for me to puzzle over:
long dead relatives

who could not have been living
at Gianna's Home Relief address.

Does she understand
enough English to answer

questions properly?
Or does she equivocate

to confuse the information-taker,
the next best thing to silence.

Old, Old Country

Born in Bedonia, Lucia, my father's mother,
was not Sicilian. Simply the bearer

of more Arab ancestry from another branch
of a cloaked lineage.

A scallop-edged photograph of her
Guinea features goes missing

from a pile spread on a table
at the end of a funeral and burial day.

A brother and I remember seeing it,
handling it, studying it. A sister-in-law

removes the clarity
to spare her children

I'm guessing
to whom

the truth will be born later.

Immigrant Haberdasher

Lucia's husband makes hats.

He prospers at a time when men
in suits went nowhere without them.

He thins under a collarless shirt
as he dies. Once robust, his heavy wool pants

float on suspenders over drooping shoulders.
But he smiles like a man well-fed

and cared for all his life, held in awe
by his many children.

Waked at home, double doors
on the brownstone parlor floor open

to the textured stone steps and waiting hearse.
Wife and daughters sob.

His brother mourns stoically,
ready to inherit the marital bed.

Liz

Liz injected her
mother's insulin shots and
    tended her diabetic feet
with a razor blade.

Youngest of three
    daughters, caretaking intimacy
came naturally.

Blood and bile held
    the older sisters fast together.

Liz died before the others,
    who did not forgive her

being favored by traditional duty
    as last-born girl
grooming her mother's body.

Liz's own ailments and
    impatience with backyard gossip
made her think she was special,

the older sisters believed.
    They held their guilty
mistake against her,

attending her funeral,
    but not the food and
drink spread following

or the parceling of rings,
    necklaces, pins, and watches.
Wood jewelry boxes empty

after the day's undertakings.
    A lawyer came in evening
to accommodate my flight schedule.

Primo, as oldest male,
    served shot glasses of Scotch
to the men present

and to me. I forgave him
    everything for that,
proud of his knowing

what to do as the ranking
    male. But I, first born,
fled next day not willing

to inherit my place
    except for ceremony
to honor blood history.

Here and There

Raised in Brooklyn blocks of Syrians
Lebanese Sicilians Puerto Ricans Italians,

Liz stands deep enough
in the cement-gray surf at Coney Island

to avoid being toppled
by breaking waves. Across the Atlantic

on the tip-of-her-eye,
the second floors of shacks

lean over dirt passage ways,
almost touch in the air

obscuring sunlight. She escapes
the Arab quarter of Palermo

dragging poverty like a net
full of treasures.

Paper Trail

A man and woman claim me
on other birth records;

on the original watermarked paper
I come alone.

A name
foreign to me, sex assigned

equally foreign.
No small footprint stains

other documents or adds
indelible burdens I am given.

Folding frays certainty. Words are fickle.
Tell outright lies confuse distort

hint. I parse them every day
and will never have the last one.

Sleep Map

A dresser drawer softened with towels.
Then toddling to aunts and cousins
on makeshift mattresses lining linoleum floors
or to kitchen chairs roped together. Wandering half-naked
to warm vacancies, I learned to sleep where I fell.

Many beds later
anxious to find a way to privacy
I turn to avoid arms cramping and turn again
forearm protecting eyes from nothing visible
in the dark. Stopped face down a chalk silhouette, knee bent.

Mismatching map folds. One-way creases.
The route shreds at critical junctures
in deserted cities. And I've been lost
for years before I sense danger.

If You Must Speak

Say "American" when asked nationality.
Some countries of origin never mention.

Every family has its hierarchy of ancestors
remembers half-truths, invents, omits,

imagines, justifies. Some forgetting is forever.
Some itches until blood lines show.

Unlearn a mother's first language
forbidden at home and a father's adopted one.

The first-born of this strategy grew up
a foot in each grave.

Now I am the truth
I see fit.

Guinea

    Chalked sidewalks
    Double-Dutch
    Rubber band handballs
    Home-made skate boxes
    Sewer cover stickball bases.

A shoe slid through spittle
    to mark the line of scrimmage
    for touch football.

Olive and brown
    hairy backs arms and chests
    washed at kitchen sinks.
    Sleeveless undershirts.
    Alley pepper, tomato plants,
    oregano, basil
    in Medalio D'Oro coffee cans.

Young husbands slept
    alone on fire escapes
    during sultry August nights.

Five-stories hand-scrubbed
    wash flapped on backyard lines
    attached to telephone poles.

Women owned the stoops.
My grandmother's lips
    sucked her toothless gums
    hands folded on her belly;
    Home Relief money
    safe against her bosom.

Corseted under a housedress,
    my mother cleaned
    Primo's ears with a hairpin,
    or raked my hair for lice
    while I was mortified in English.

All the mothers are lost in translation.

Caravans of over-stuffed cars
    drove Sunrise Highway
    from Red Hook to fields of corn,
    potatoes, strawberries.

They settled embryonic towns:
    Wantagh, Seaford,
    Massapequa. Native dead
    turned over in our foundation stones.

I was a plump olive girl
    shamed by nuns snapping rods.
    Public school classmates
    giggled at my name.

I made my way to brainy Rosenthal
    thick glasses, red hair as fuzzy as mine,
    enough chest for both of us.

To the only Black girl in class
    Zorrida who slept with her boyfriend
    when she was ten. Her white mother
    slept with him too.

With them I made my restricted way
    though Wonder Bread lunch rooms,
    through halls mined with ugly words.

With them I made my way.

House Storm

No one noticed
the tarpaper roof leaks in the garage—
    filled ceiling to floor with rotting
    orphaned miscellany—
    pulley door panels, warped and separating.

Flanking a paved entry, wood flower boxes
sagged and leaked bleached splinters and dry dirt.
Purple pansies slid askew.

What flourished were old cars—
    first repaired to give their final months
    of service, then retired to a side yard,
    picked clean of serviceable parts.

The not-quite-American mother of the house
sat behind the wheel of each junker in turn,
one hand on the steering wheel,
elbow on the glassless window frame.

No one noticed
a tuneless upright piano in the living room
played only during losses of electricity.

The father, bare-chested over the keys.
Children in darkness descended from attic rooms.
The mother abandoned her kitchen window vigil.

No one noticed
a family without power sharing darkness
and listening to off-key music,
thunder, blood closing ranks.

Yogi

You were a taciturn man
    carrying a spade on your shoulder,
    a handgun on your belt, and
you regularly killed
    your limit of whatever was in season.

You walked a familiar wood for the last time
    with a feeble Labrador
    whose long companionship
    you could not let a stranger's needle
terminate.

The dog retched near the ground where you dug,
    but you no longer checked his sickness for blood.

You tucked his sleeping blanket
    into the wide, deep hole.

Did he come as called, obedient to the grave?

I see you knee-deep in the earth
    stretching to cradle and pull him in

curled at your feet
    before the *coup de grâce*.

Auld Lang Syne

A new year morning
after an all-night party,

family asleep everywhere,
their overcoats as blankets.

We leave for home. Her Rambler
crushes fresh snow where Liz parks

in first light of day. Heater
blasts, radio music

moves from night to day. We stay
in the warm cocoon.

They stink, Liz says of my Camel.
She favors L&Ms, a hard filtered draw.

We smoke mesmerized
listening to flute notes

of Swingin' Shepherd
Blues. Together. Once. At ease.

Hooked Semitic Nose

Hooked Semitic nose, tight black curls,
upper arms as thick as thighs, hands like dark puff pastry.
    That one shoulda been a boy,
Aunt Mary said, editing my mother's mockery—
correctly translated—*She thinks she has a dick.*

Aunt Mary had a slow albino daughter who
people mistook for my mother's child,
my mother a desert color. I was olive
like Aunt Mary and had her hooded lids.

    Both sisters ruled with their eyes,
a kick under the table, a hand shaking air.
They cracked cheeks and swung brooms and straps.

Between them they ridiculed
being too fat or too skinny, too brown or too pale,
hair too straight or too curly, noses too big or too little.

    Aunt Mary beat her un-marriageable daughter
into a life of household servitude—
fearing for her the dangers outside.

Only when I refused to stop
wearing the neckties my mother used to choke me,
only when I was callused by her protection,
did she let me slip beyond her into America
to commit the crime of my life.

But for having withstood her, silently,
from a distance, she tossed me the dregs of her love,
and with that blessing I left home forever. Her offspring.

INDIGESTIBLE MEMORIES

Weathered

East coast hurricane
    hurricane child
    child of a child.

Police logs for queers
    named her at fourteen.

Gin clouded high school
    and college stealing
    books to study.

Acid-soaked pot
    blew her into tornado cellars.
Midwest blizzards
    whited-out hemorrhaging ridicule.

The nadir of cross-country storming:
    west coast fog. Finally,

desert winds scorched
    sand and waves wrinkling.

Alumnae Class of '64

Radicals, rebels, brainiacs, and bad girls
smoked in a windowless room—
a women's Catholic college, in loco parentis
it claimed. We reeked of tobacco.

Dummy Bridge players rolled paper
into portable Olympias to continue writing
someone's paper due. Theological drivel
in many voices.

Mostly, we attended classes. Avid
for history, anthropology,
literature, and philosophy.
Civil rights and justice, writ large.

Aquinas required of us. *Nausea*,
Tropic of Cancer, *Death on the Installment Plan*—
impossible to hide from us. Learning:
hypocrisy was the law of the land.

A few popped benies. Un-Mary-like
others kept pints of J&B in their purses.
No one knew which friends or lovers
would be untimely dead.

We pictured each
other decades later as twenty-one-year-olds,
all promise and eternity ahead.

Golden Gate

Sprawled on foul territory in the park,
    I rooted for the team with more black

and brown players. Game cliches with other
    loners exercised vocal cords otherwise

in danger of atrophying. Once, near the Music
    Concourse, I sat in a parked car; a police

cruiser pulled up behind. A white cop, cupped
    his holstered gun like adjusting his balls,

walked toward the driver's side. When he
    returned to his vehicle to call in

the registration and driver's IDs—uniform a skin
    on his back—I left the passenger side

casually with real and imagined things
    to hide. My skin color and

papers not quite in order.
    Into a nearby group, I passed.

Loaded Words

For P.P.

Bourbon poet
in the ink of California
escaped her deacon father
given to laying on hands.

Black bourbon sweat
poet writing off friends
not wise enough to love her
belligerent angry brilliance.

Creating alibis for thirsty ghost,
bourbon-eyed poet ingratiates
at public readings. Ordinary people
appreciate her staged words.

A heady victory for bourbon lusting
poet. Frantic without a steady blond
fortress against collection notices
domestic disorderly drop-in

victims of companionable addictions.
Bourbon head doses with wanton soup
after triple movie feature afternoons
killing time drying out every first day

declared last drop.

Business Tripping

A minefield of backstories from the airport
to downtown San Francisco,

about the former life she died there,
walking day and night, exhausting vitality

*for ten years. Brokenhearted, sure,
but something more*

deadly. Miles of erasure.
Then as seamless as witness protection

make-believe, she walks into a pricey hotel
and slaps down an American Express corporate card.

Wasting no sunshine, she walks to South of Market
places now gentrified like her. Folsom Street

*once housed a storefront collective
that served rice, beans and vegetables*

*for one dollar. When yellow
tape closed them, she didn't know where*

the next cheap meal would come from.
Slippery subterranean to a sunny sidewalk

café table. Pastry and espresso. Anytime
backwash of prematurely dead women of color

from her ragtag group. Some escaped obituaries,
police blotters, ten-year benders.

§

Lofty windows reflect professional
faker in hotel robe drinking Scotch,

checking messages from another time zone,
a shadow life coming and going.

She dresses dark for reception and stands
wine and cheese for the hour it takes

to let colleagues look at her, so butch
brown won't be a shock next morning,

when sweat ruins the red silk blouse
under her presentation kick-ass suit.

§

Evening scotch in the lobby bar with a local
friend. Fresh lipstick and perfume

brighten her life-after-death day as chancellor
of a Bay Area college. They laugh at high level

absurdities—squelched until their meeting—
neither has female colleagues in their rarified ranks.

A carafe of red over dinner dulls daily indigestion.
Chancellor describes her black heartburn as the face

of downsizing faculty only recently diversified.
Mortified, she accepted the prestigious appointment

without grasping its cynical underbelly,
which will compromise her one way or another.

§

Last minute conference business at breakfast,
dealing more embossed cards, even as the title

on them free-falls. Her mask cracks
during the drive to the airport bar—

Sunday afternoon football in every corner,
mercifully muted like the weekend fading.

Aloft, she swirls scotch; mulls hopes
for perfumed chancellor on her own nova.

Business drag stored overhead. She dreams
and wakes. Dreams and wakes. Low life

mid-life. Crisis quaking.

"Ladies and Gentlemen,
we have begun our descent."

SF/ABQ

A thundering
    split / second
monsoon Albuquerque
    pours / on sea level gloom.

Blinding rain outside.
Winter mudslides / hurry underground,
slippery transitions.
    Wet leaves
    wind-blown on BART steps /

arrive drenched
    in sunlight arroyos
rushing me over
ground / flowing
    with re-born time.

Torch Song

A holdover from the twentieth century,
I drive to the smoky Sheraton lounge

where Linda Cotton covers the standards.

Before she gets to a foggy London town,
a conference crowd talks and table hops.

It's pointless to glare at them.

But she quiets us all when she gets to
I can't make you love me.

I'm not thinking about romantic love.

I can't make the world love *me*
is what I'm really thinking

a needle stuck in an LP groove.

The heart of the night she shows me—
invisible in the spotlight of *her* gig—

I can't make you love me
when only one or two are listening

on a Scotch and soda night.

Figment

I phoned my mother
after being out of touch
for years. She asked me

if I had been in prison.
I had not, but was slyly

pleased she thought so low
of me. I was her daughter
after all, and loved her

from a stiff-arm distance—
continentally divided.

What she was telling
me about ancestral depths
is this: I am the rapist,
torturer, monstrously
sadistic perpetrator

in my fretful mind. I am
a figment of my own
thigh-high mindless garbage
passing through.

Cloak

Remember the thrill
    of a man's jacket
of arms slipping into the sleeves

and fitting over a female body—
    wool heavy enough to disguise
a camisole against your skin—

a magic cloak to fly you
    to your country.
Add a tie smartly knotted

practiced before a mirror
    behind closed doors
and step into the world

if you dare
    leave home. Eventually,
you dressed as you pleased;

the laws changed
    and men's overcoats
on women became a fashion

statement, not an identity.
    Cross-dressing did not cover
who wore the clothes,

did not make the man.
    Or the woman
could not hide the physical

contradictions. Being
    the problem no wardrobe would
correct without drastic alterations

that even so would not shroud
    the hole buried
    in the body.

Remedial Science

Baseballs curve against expectation,
but so do I draped in a woman's body
transfer energy against expectation.

If charge is a property of matter
where do poetry and physics
become scientific phrasemaking?

Remember *The Tao of Physics*,
The Dancing Wu Li Masters?
A generation fascinated by science

for lay people. Don't read critically
because every day I love you
less. That's entropy. Disorder

always increases in closed systems,
and I am tightly boxed in here.
My serotonin re-uptake

inhibitor epitomizes remedial
science, but still I fall faster
the closer I am to collapse.

Doctor Illusions

Comatose relationships, dismal prognoses,
after a series of organic failures,
systems of pleasure and trust compromised,
when do not resuscitate would be a kindness,
    I use heroic measures to keep love alive.
I transplant artificial vital signs and perform
costly and invasive acts against love's demise.

Early on I told women what they wanted to hear,
what they deserved to hear,
and never outgrew playing doctor.
But even truth cloys in repetition.
Once subversive praises now drip as morphine.

Doctor Illusions works miracles for mutual coma.

Touching

Your heart falls short
of soft flesh under my hand
fingers stirring your need

and mine to kneel in welcome
to be desired
for passion in hand

carried home for your pleasure:
a physical unity not an idea,
not a memory.

But impulses misfire
even mentally. Nerve ends
cauterized by drugs to smooth edges

of me touching you—defeated
before any *effort* to pioneer
    a new refuge through rusted desire.

Clueless

Forgive my being
so sure of my ways and means,
of my opinions
a know-it-all, often wrong.
About me and you and what

we notice. Forgive
the clueless man lurking in
my tool kit. Subtle
feelings foreign and scary,
Unnecessary trouble.

Forgive my being
hard on self-discovery
tropes of Fifties women
and men cramped into boxes
clueless of alternatives.

Indigestible Memories

Eating alone in fast food
    dive
long gone indigestible memories

mouth and belly stuffed
five fries at a time.

What did I think
    nostalgia would taste like?
Given the age of my stomach and intestines.

Listen tender creature,
    weathering miles of loneliness
one foot in front of another,

nothing happened between miles
    of feeding
except temperature-controlled places to rest.

Listen tender one,
dragged through heart slums
you deserved

better for lighting
the way here.

RUINS

Haikus for Dead Friends

Too scattered
        to die.
If a pain shocks you
        present,
feel the chest
        thumping.

§

Airless sharp
        breathing
escapes chilly wind.
        Practice
anchor drops away.

§

Bright sheets   dim
        waiting
Loved-one bearing
        solution
for going
        beyond.

Buried

Skeletal fingers scratch sand.
    Grains spill time back onto desert
floor. Familiar terrain but

vague: Saharan, Arabian,
    Kalahari. My fingers
touch bones and scoop free the rib

cage. Remains sit upright; femur,
    fibula, and tibia
stacked from sitting on haunches

in a hole. Other forensic
    markings on the skull: fractures
and shattering. I feel her

panicked pulse and juddering
    heart before the first stone hits
me awake in my sweaty bed.

Nakba

I sit in ruins
thousands of miles away
dead bodies stifle my breathing
air that others cannot
swallow from harm witnessed
thousands of miles away.
Stop slaughtering the earth
stone bread and crushed cradles.
Breathe above the stinking rubble
thousands of miles away
witness the reeking catastrophe.

WhatsApp

From an article
about being powerless

in America
to cousins calling from Afghanistan.

The callers brutalized by Taliban
hear *there is nothing we can do*

we have no influence
as indifference.

And that is merely one
WhatsApp family

dreading communiques
from Gaza, the Sudan, and Congo.

What other line can possibly go with this?

Rubble

Mortar blows off an
apartment wall, the same floor
plan in each unit
beds tilt down and fall from use.
A stout lone woman walks down

the hill of rubble,
to which she had returned for
her mother's egg cup
cracked but gilded, clutched in hand,
a family memento.

Head scarf tied under
chin, she concentrates on each
step taken and on
each precious walking breath she
feels pulsing in bravery.

The Chair

A woman, gray hair
escaping from under her
kerchief, sits on a
wooden chair near a rural
road; no others in sight, weeds,

brush stripped of summer.
Black coat hunches her shoulders.
A blue throw covers
her knees. Lined face suggests
the impromptu convoy might

not return for her
and the small white garbage bag
of possessions on
the ground beside her. They might
have squeezed her in. Instead, they

left a chair for her:
to huddle alone with prayers:
Scandinavian
silent movie image with-
out subtitles or color.

Texas Pastor

Speechlessly, I watch
Texas pastor interviewed
for organizing
Ukrainian refugee
relief supplies. His people

stack and sort canned and
dry goods, soap and socks. He's asked
if his effort marks
a change in American
altruism. Yes, he says. We

need to step up when
people are in need, or there's
a political
crisis. In the TV frame,
a sign points to Mexico.

The accidental
irony does not trouble
the pastor. He has
not seen black or brown faces
suffering political

violence. It looks
different he might say if you
questioned him. Closer.
lately, a classroom of young
Texas students were gunned down.

It occurs to plain
folks: they are not safe in church
in the grocery
store, at the mall. Their kids are
not safe at their desks. No one

is safe in their own
living room. They become more
vigilant, wary.
Black people and brown model
living with the threat daily.

Triangle

Black Angus on my side
    a two-lane mountain road
talks back when I tell it to go home.
    It pees where it stands in a free-range state.

My equilibrium wobbles
    annoyed by online requests for money.
People ask for donations
    at traffic intersections

with cardboard signs. Not as part of
    online panhandling. A mood

down-shifts.
    Brown woman in Taco Cabana
    emphasizes her pique to a companion,

first in her shoulders, up through her neck,
    then head—ethnic inflection

in her vibratory system. I smile
    at the quesadilla *triangle* at my lips.

Troubled Sleep Ghazal

Troubled sleep is a national disgrace. No more violence,
please. There must be somewhere calm living space. No more violence.

Daily, policemen who wake up on the wrong side of the dead,
pollute the eye and prevent human grace. No more violence.

Psychological questionnaires for lawmen should inquire
if shooting black-skinned folks is commonplace. No more violence.

Cops watch the same news programs as others see, but they ignore
the finger pointing at their guilty face. No more violence.

Millions of primetime witnesses cannot convince patriots
Blues' depravity infects the broad base. No more violence.

Midnight name cannot find a quirky twist. Hatred won't age out.
Madmen foul the water without a trace. No more violence.

GOOD LIFE IN HARD TIMES

Tennis at Winter's Edge

On the courts thirty degrees
this morning, the sun low and slow

rising over the Sandia Mountains,
but it is shining. Down and thermal

come off after the first set. Fingers cold,
but ungloved on the dominant hand.

The same Monday foursome
for years—all surnamed Tennis

in my phone contacts. Walking to
and from courts we've learned

who is widowed; has an ailing spouse;
marrying off a grandkid;

waiting on test results.
All formidable once; now

losing our edge with every
major illness and recovery.

We don't sit during change-overs
nor do we chat between sets.

We *play*, though aging
out of competition. No-ad

at deuce to save old rotator cuffs.
Any ball beyond sensible effort,

we call a good shot!
Our court coverage even for doubles

diminishes as we do.
We will never live

to open all the Dunlaps we own.
But we rotate partners while we can.

Midnight Stop

Driving the dark mesa
    toward glitter
    valley night lights,
    illumined buildings,
    ebony mountains faint

in moonless pitch—A flash
    senseless joy brakes the car.
    On the road shoulder,
    deep breathing

    disappearing.

Mesas and Canyons

From an ancestral
birth cry, I made a habit
of woe, protecting
inherited disgrace. I
retired all of it

in these historic
mesas and canyons: nature
aging in place with
me, and a woman I'd dreamed
fitting me with her own scars:

both delivered to
healing enchantment late in
life: embarrassing
change of fortune—living well—
given the backstory odds.

Fire Danger

Seventy-mile-per-
hour winds scream through Rio
Grande corridor.
I drive from Albuquerque
in patches of blinding gusts.

Two hands on the wheel.
En route, no fallen boulders
or trees block access
to the Jemez Mountains, where
I overlook the mesas.

The living room scene
shows Sylvie's salvage efforts:
deck chairs, tables, grill,
compost tubs—misplaced beyond
their control hurled then hurried

indoors. The old grill
went airborne, Sylvie says. Its
side panels lifted
like metal wings then slammed down,
scattering askew wheels, hood, and

vents. Oily fragments
from last year cooking outside
cover the deck with
potential fuel to connect
the dots. Local newscaster

reports wild fire near
Jemez Springs. No containment
in these conditions.
We wait for news to clear out

follow smoke plumes in
the sky and on the TV
screen. Maybe a downed
power line sparked and dragon
tongue devoured more acres.

The suffocating
smoke spares us engulfs others.

Scotch and Buddha

Two fingers of Scotch.
Staring at Buddha in bronze.
What is there without
ice cubes and Chivas? Alone
with poetry now. Wind, wild

fires occupy
New Mexico. One after
another pine tree
burns to wasted energy.
Before climate change crisis

we worried about
living with weapons of mass
destruction one mile
from downtown Albuquerque
in Kirtland Air Force Base. Now,

deeper in the high
desert. A new destruction.
Did ponderosas
know fire was coming? Could they
bargain with dragons and wind?

Elements surely
signal to each other, if
we listen in. They
show no respect, they say, for
man(un)kind despoiling.

White Horse

Every morning I
prepare coffee for Sylvie
and me—something of
a sacrament—I survey
the valley occupants through

kitchen windows. At
the ranch where a white horse boards,
in a separate
field, an unusual sight:
a small herd of cattle. They

evacuated
from the voracious fire,
the largest in the
country, north of my vantage.
The State Fair Grounds is among

sites also open
to threatened livestock, so what
I see below must
be a private arrangement
to give safety and feed to

the displaced creatures.
My chest hums for all beings
involved in this gift:
earthly generosity
and the reward of seeing

it. The closest ranch
is for black cows bred for meat
we think, though Sylvie
and I get sentimental
over every calf. We don't

say "a calf." We say,
"little cow." Probably, the
animals are not
aware of us. But we're sure
the mesas we face know us.

Holidays

A thousand miles off
my Sylvie is. Missing her
at arms distance. We
have another week apart.
She will be with Passover

friends. Passover is
close to Easter this year. I
celebrate neither.
"Ramadan Mubarak" I
say. Lamb shawarma and hummus

dinner boxed to go.
Middle Eastern restaurant
closing early for
the family meal at sundown.
Abrahamic coincidence.

Space Junk

While you were away,
I used your coffee mug. My
transgressive impulse
blooms in my heart. Scooping stars
out of debris and snapping

blankets free of dust
particles in the air are
survival gestures.
The empty self I turn to
face you reflects space junk. May

this reality
soup—dim... then glow, revealing
no bowl or spoon, no
hungry ego ghost to nurse
massive and fragile awake.

Los Ojos

Sylvie has a jones
for Los Ojos's burgers and
onion rings. We drive
into Jemez Springs—to one
of the best saloons in the

USA—Bach on
the radio. We're like that.
The saloon comes with
country music oldies—we
appreciate them also

mounted long guns on
the walls, huge antlers over
the mantle. Cowboy
nostalgia in signage and
artifacts. Sylvie and I

are aware of land
not ceded. We open a
cell phone game; the wait
is worse during the second
year of the pandemic. We

order. Snapping flames
toast and lull us. No word games
necessary. Food
arrives in baskets; waitress
brings a fistful of napkins

without our asking.
Soaking in fireplace heat and
twang southwestern fare
sweet and salty memories
of other indulgences.

Summer Squash

Summer squash brought by
our neighbor to the door. He
often brings buckets
of wild or cultivated
flowers he grows to take to

weekend market, where
Sylvie chats with locals and
buys their eggs and greens.

Sometimes expensive
Bodhi Zen yogurt. I hold
space for villagers—
good people, I imagine—
and seldom see. They go to

Christian church. Favor
liberal causes without
messy conflict. They

genuinely care
for mirrored white faces, but
restrict their caring,
unaware of worlds beyond
polite discussion. I try

conversation in
their territory, sadness
mixed in for not all

to see me. In the
beginning was the weather
exciting the sky.
Pouring lush growth on
the earth. Wonders came mending.

Cold Mountain Morning

Hands around the hot
coffee mug, plants, animals
minerals, I thank,
elements, and humans for
caffeine and for our daily

nourishment. Seven
inches of snow freezing all
day and night. Mountains
watch me watch un-blanketed
horses and milk cows below.

Constant gratitude
works its way into locals
and into the world
I retired from. Wearing
flannel pajamas, I read

a passage from Thây,
then push ink on a notebook
page, loving fountain
pen and paper. Intention
for my well-being, also

the well-being of
others. I check my cell phone,
laptop, where I greet
other contemplatives confined
to zoom squares: live-stock corralled.

Al Fresco

The sun sheds warm rays
this January morning.

Sylvie and I in
sleeping bags protected for
al fresco meditation.

We look like cruise ship
passengers idling on deck
chairs. No ocean waves

below, only livestock to
watch us grazing in our lives.

On a Beach in Mazatlán

breezy dragons sway
in sky-framed palm fronds.
Foamy chaos crowns wave after wave
crash and ebb.

Where *exactly* in my eye is water sand?
Do sea and sky touch on the horizon?
And along the wet surface
from sand to water to sky:
where does difference begin and end?

Do I breathe mystery under my nose?
Air to skin? Is all I think threshold?
Seeing water am I sand?

I am all chaos imagining distinctions.

LIFE LINES

Iberian Scribe

In another time and place,
    days passed inking words.

No inspiration was needed
    Simply the quill

shushing rhythmically.
    Sacramental plagiarism.

Daily I lived in a carrel
    among other writers

breathing nearby vellum
    I use as needed,

liquid gold or silver ink.
    I lived with words,

preserving antiquity,
    philosophy, history—

intoxicated on ink—
    like a Sufi dancer

practicing an alphabet
    etched in consciousness

Routine

A colleague thinks
there is purpose

in writing poems
for others to read.

I write to watch words
appear on the page.

I welcome readers,
need them, but ambition

is window-dressing on indulgence.

Every morning from the deck,
I count horses and cows

Is that poetry? Really,
does someone counting

livestock invite dismissal?

The joy of this desk business
is trusting

that after writing whatever
comes to mind, a different ink

will cull the dreck.

Pens and Inks

I have more pens and inks than words.
Arranging them absorbs the hand-eye skill
of doodling poems on a page.

I wish the pens were full of themselves.
I wish the rosewood sticks
and various nibs wrote their own stories
with my fingers.

The disorder of second guessing
is what a work page looks like.
Disorder gives as much pleasure
as the instruments of music or surgery
or every pursuit *in media res*.

Arriving at the coffin of completion
the effort framed after free-wheeling
red or brown corrective blots and lines
of travel from one stanza to another.

Finally, a signature
pen that is out of ink.

Wet Ink

A nib shushes
tooth of paper

wet ink line
curves loops

measured shapely
mounds descents:

a cursive community
pleasurably verbose.

A new pen practices
a name I go by.

Contrails

A resin Adirondack chair
    on the broad arm

a tumbler of watered-down Jack
    sample from memory

other people's methods
    for making a mark

riffing
    some sources sui generis

only black ink
    on foolscap:

contrails in the evening sky

Like an Ass

> *"Like an ass laden with books."*
> —Rumi quoting the Qur'an

They know my name. See
the dunce cap teetering on
a mountain of books:
stubborn concepts, ideas a
wasteland of confusion.

Wish it gone, but must
be lying when I say that,
or it would be gone.
O gaté, gaté. Another self-
cherishing desire.

LAGNIAPPE

Graveyard Relatives

My brother and I follow confusing signs
    through acres of memorial stones
in a sprawling Long Island graveyard.

Bearded, bald, helmeted, he
    leans into circles of misdirection;
I look around his neck and shoulders.

He keys off the Harley and drops the kickstand
    in front of a building
where his twenty-something
    daughter assists a manager

who marks the silent occupants present each day.
She wants to meet me, East for a rare visit.

Brother and I don't want to go inside
the building—too spooky among the living.

We remove our helmets in three-digit
heat and wait for the her to come outside.

"This is my daughter." He is beaming.
    "This is your..." He hesitates
then gives my name,
    avoiding the gender specific aunt or uncle.

The girl and I try not to stare at each other
    and struggle with chit chat.

No one dares suggest a meal together
    much less a day or a weekend
to get to know one another.

I've only recently connected
    with my brother who was a baby
when I left home.

I'll probably never see the girl again,
    or him, but we had our Harley ride

in the cemetery, which will tell better
    than it lived, about three of us

who carried the family loner DNA
    to employment among the dead

and a twenty-minute family reunion
    among dumb gray stones.

Mediterranean Coast

From Cairo
out of my tourist way

I bus to Alexandria and trade
Durrell's colonial version of Egypt

for Mahfouz's alleys of origin.
The truth: I live more in written words

than in cities anywhere.

Observing the custom of friends
walking arm-in-arm with Helen

along the Mediterranean coast
or in the palace park—our skin colors

local—other couples
and groups observing Friday

greet us as close to home
as I will ever be.

Not a Trace

Stand at dusk in a
field of seven-foot cordgrass.
Without breaking the
stems, sweep a handful over-
head and braid strands with a near-

by cluster. Turning
as center pole, continue
sweeping and braiding
in the ten directions. When
you release the last handful,

grass billows above
you. Shelter and sit until
light comes in morning.
Undo your threads, leaving no
sign of communion and place.

Acknowledgments

"Here and There" first appeared in a slightly different version in the chapbook *Weathered* and in *Harwood Anthology*.

"Guinea" first appeared in a slightly different version in the chapbook *Rumi's Falcon* and in *Spinsters Ink*.

"Touching" first appeared in *Adobe Walls*.

"Hooked Semitic Nose" first appeared in a slightly different version in the chapbooks *Rumi's Falcon* and *Weathered*.

"Business Tripping," "Weathered," "Alumnae Class of '64," "House Storm," "Sleep Map," "If You Must Speak," "Wet Ink," and "Paper Trail," in slightly different versions, first appeared in the chapbook *Weathered*.

"SF/ABQ," "Yogi," and "Torch Song" first appeared in slightly different versions in the chapbook *Rumi's Falcon*.

"Loaded Words" first appeared in a slightly different version in the chapbook *Poems in Thin Air*.

"Los Ojos" first appeared in a slightly different version in *After the Thunder* and *One Albuquerque, One Hundred Poets*.

About the author

DODICI AZPADU is a gender queer, American-born Sicilian Arab. They live with their Jewish spouse in New Mexico, where they practice Shalom Bayit (Peace in the House). Recently, Azpadu has come out of retirement to teach a master class in fiction writing at the University of New Mexico.

Their novel *Living Room* was a finalist for the Lambda Literary Award, the Golden Crown Literary Award, and the New Mexico Book Award. In 2025, they published *Dead of Winter*, a historical fiction novel about the underbelly of the women's movement in the 1970s.

The Margaret Randall Poetry Series

THE MARGARET RANDALL POETRY SERIES showcases and celebrates poets from around the world. The volumes in the series, selected and published by Casa Urraca Press, honor the ongoing legacy of author Margaret Randall, known for her gifts with language and her passion for lifting the voices of poets and other creatives.

Margaret Randall is a poet, essayist, oral historian, translator, photographer, and social activist, and the author of more than two hundred books. She lived in Latin America for twenty-three years (in Mexico, Cuba, and Nicaragua); from 1962 to 1969, she co-edited *El Corno Emplumado / The Plumed Horn*, a bilingual literary quarterly that published some of the best new literature and art of the sixties. When she came home in 1984, the government ordered her deported because it found some of her writing to be "against the good order and happiness of the United States." With the support of many writers and others, she won her case and her citizenship was restored in 1989.

Randall lives in Albuquerque, New Mexico, with her wife, artist Barbara Byers. She continues to write and travels extensively to read, lecture, and teach, championing her fellow poets along the way.

Casa Urraca Press

Casa Urraca Press publishes creative nonfiction, poetry, fiction, and other works by authors we believe in. New Mexico and the U.S. Southwest are rich in creative and literary talent, and the rest of the world deserves to experience our perspectives. So we champion books that belong in the conversation—books with the power, compassion, and variety to bring very different people closer together.

We were founded in the high desert somewhere near Abiquiú, New Mexico. Visit us at casaurracapress.com to read more from our authors, browse all editions of our books, and register for writing workshops and retreats.